Michael All About Me

Written by Michael Rosen   **Illustrated by Tim Archbold**

Contents

 Collins

Our family lived in a flat in a place called Pinner, in a road called Love Lane. When we had to tell the class our address, me saying "Love Lane" always used to get a good giggle.

This is the bus stop we waited at to get to the swimming pool.

me and my brother Brian at Pinner station

Pinner at that time was what's called a "London suburb". That meant it wasn't the kind of place where there were lots of factories, but it wasn't out in the country either. It was really halfway between the two. Once it had been a village, and then at the beginning of the 20th century, a railway was built connecting it to London and straight away lots of houses were built.

Oh yes, I remember this: it was where you could get anything from dustbins to paraffin lamps.

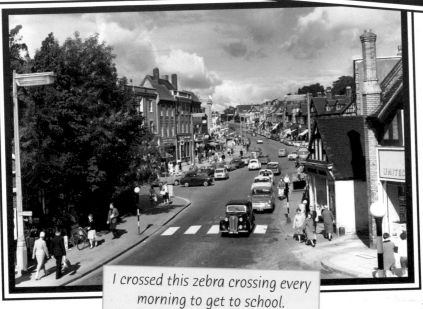

I crossed this zebra crossing every morning to get to school.

3

The railway was part of what we now call the London Underground and the line to Pinner was the Metropolitan line. You can see it on the map of the London Underground.

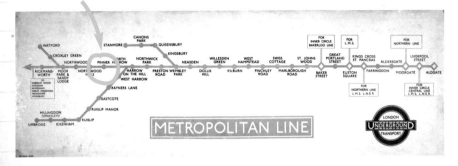

The trains were divided up into compartments (like little cabins). In each compartment there was a brass plate next to the train door handle and written in curly writing on it was, "Live in Metro Land". I often used to wonder about how I was living in "Metro Land".

Pinner station a bit before my time!

Family life

Our flat was above an estate agent, and I lived with my mum, dad, brother, and for a while when I was young, a friend of my dad's called Brian. Brian had the room behind the shop. Upstairs there was a "front room" over the shop, a study, a bathroom and a kitchen. Upstairs again was my parents' room at the front, and the one shared by me and my brother at the back.

On holiday with my brother Brian and my mum and dad: I'm in the hat!

the front room of our flat

5

Having an older brother was like having a third parent. He took it on himself to bring me up. Whatever he learnt, he felt that he had to tell me about it. When I was 11 and he was 15, he was doing something called Calculus, which is this really, really, really hard Maths – it's so hard you can't believe it – and he used to sit there, trying to explain it to me.

me and Brian when we were young

But we also had a lot of fun: when we shared a bedroom, he would spend hours and hours putting on performances, pretending to be my mum and my dad, or teachers at school.

Of course we didn't always get on, and I think he sometimes thought I was a bit spoilt. I certainly didn't get told off nearly as much as he did.

Harrybo and me

From the age of about seven, Harrybo was my main pal. He lived at the end of my road and we just hung out together all the time.

Sometimes we'd explore the countryside – the woods, the farm and the river Pinn, which we would walk along for miles. We'd spend hours playing with the stuff people used to throw into the river, like old bikes and prams. Or we'd go "**ponding**" and try to catch tadpoles, newts and frogs.

We had hours of fun on the river Pinn.

Sometimes we'd go towards the "towny" bit, which is called Wealdstone and Harrow, and go to the swimming baths and the chip shop, and hang about in the streets.

There were two guys who used to stand outside Harrow and Wealdstone station selling newspapers – a great big bloke and a little tiny bloke – and the great big bloke used to say, "Nah new an nan nah," which actually meant "*Star, News* and *Standard*". These were the names of the three newspapers he was selling, but you couldn't really tell. Then the little bloke next to him would say, in a deep gruff voice, "Ay ah!" and that meant "*Late Star*". So they'd stand there outside the station, taking it in turns to say their words. Harrybo and I thought this was hysterically funny, so we used to stand on the other side of the road and imitate them:
"Nah new an nan nah," and
"Ay ah!" Of course we
got chased off.

Harrybo and I read books at the same time and then talked about them. After reading the two Winnie the Pooh books, I can remember we walked along the road together singing, "My nose is cold-tiddley-pom."

At school

I went to two primary schools and two secondary schools. The second primary school, which I went to between the ages of seven and 11, had just been built – a brand new school, with a big playground. I was in a class of about 48 children. We all sat in rows of desks, four rows of 12.

My class, Year Five: I'm at the back with the very short haircut.

I was no good at all at Maths, but I loved writing stories and anything to do with animals. I once took photos of the ducks in the park and wrote a little piece about each photo, and the teacher put it up on the wall. I was very proud of that.

Mallards, 1956

On Fridays, our head teacher used to come into our class and read us a chapter from a book called *Hue and Cry*, about some children who spent their days on the bomb sites in London just after the war. I absolutely adored hearing this story and we used to plead with our head teacher to read more than one chapter, but he always kept us on tenterhooks till the next week.

Footy and swimming

I was mad keen on sport when I was at school. Football, cricket and swimming were the main sports I liked. But I wasn't very good at sport, so I was one of those kids that people didn't want to pick for the team.

Even so, I was in the school football team, and I played what we used to call centre half, which is now called central defence. I remember walking home with the football teacher, Mr Baggs, and he said, "Well you see, Mike, what you need in a football team is a real powerhouse at the centre of defence – the centre half. Really, the whole game revolves around the centre half. You have to have a really good centre half. Now, who have we got at centre half? … Oh, right, yeah …" And then it all went quiet because he remembered it was me.

Now, swimming I wasn't too bad at – I was actually very good at breast stroke, not so good at front crawl. When I was 11 we had a swimming gala, where all the different schools competed against each other at swimming. I'd been told there would be a breast stroke race, so I thought, "Great, I stand quite a good chance at this." Then, when it actually came to the swimming gala, there was only a front crawl race, but I was in the team. So, I raced breast stroke against guys doing front crawl, and I came last! My friends thought this was extremely funny and teased me about it for ages.

"Did you pass?"

When I was 11 I took an exam called the 11-plus. This decided whether you would go to the grammar school or a secondary modern school. The whole of my last two years at primary school, which are now called Years Five and Six, were full of worry about whether we would pass this exam or not.

Every week we did tests, an English test and a Maths test, and our teacher would average up the marks and put us in a place in the class according to the mark. So that meant every week we changed where we sat in the class. Now that in itself didn't matter too much: you just took your stuff out of your desk and moved. But you didn't get a chance to sit with your friends or at a table you liked. I always wanted to sit in twelfth place because the person who was twelfth always got to ring the school bell. I never was twelfth though!

I remember the day the results came, and seeing the envelope on the doormat in our flat. I didn't want to open it because I was so worried that I wouldn't pass. I did pass though, and on the way to school, everyone was calling to each other across the park, "Did you pass? Did you pass?"

I start performing

The next school I went to was a mixed grammar school for people who had passed that 11-plus exam. It was halfway up a big hill called Harrow Weald, surrounded by oak trees.

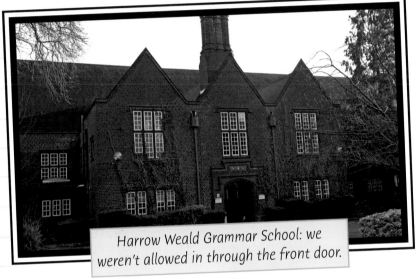

Harrow Weald Grammar School: we weren't allowed in through the front door.

I hung about in a group of boys who were all very, very funny. We loved messing around doing accents, and we used to spend hours in our breaks imitating teachers, or pretending to be people on television or in the films.

Me and my mates hanging out: I'm second from the left.

A wrong turning?

Once I got to 15, I had to take a set of exams which are now called GCSEs, and although I didn't do much Science, I did do **Biology** and I absolutely loved it. All the other subjects I was doing were Arts subjects: English, French, German, **Latin** and English **Literature**. After the exams I was going to go into the sixth form (that's like college), and I was going to do English, French and History, but I thought it was a shame to stop doing Biology, because I loved animals and plants.

When I was trying to decide what subjects to do, I happened to say to my parents about wanting to carry on with Biology as well as the Arts. So suddenly my parents, who were always desperately keen for me to do what I was interested in, said, "Maybe there's some kind of job you can do where you could keep your interest in the biological things, but at the same time carry on your interests in books and history and language – I wonder what that could be?"

We sat around and talked and somehow or other we got to the idea of me being a doctor, because a doctor knows all about how the body works and is also interested in how human beings think. So I thought, yes, this sounds right.

Before I knew what was going on, my parents were off talking to their great old friend, Dr Carter, and telling me how I could still do the English, French and History in the sixth form, and then go to medical school.

I felt like I was on a wheel that I couldn't get off. The next thing I knew, I was doing English, French and History in the sixth form, and then I went to medical school to study how to be a doctor.

So there I was, sitting in the middle of a laboratory, **dissecting** rats and looking through a very complicated machine called a **spectrometer** and I panicked! I thought, I don't really want to be doing this.

I moved to Oxford University and carried on studying to be a doctor at first, but after a year I switched and started to study English Literature and Language. That is really what I should have been doing in the first place!

Wadham College, Oxford, where I was for four years

me at university, playing the chief weasel in Toad of Toad Hall

Acting and writing

I had been obsessed, absolutely crazy about theatre, since I was about seven. My parents took me and my brother to see plays all the time. They used to put on school plays because they were teachers, and we went to all their school plays. When I was about nine all I wanted to be was an actor.

I acted a bit at school, but there wasn't much Drama so my dad found this place called the Questors Theatre in Ealing and when I was 12 I started going once a week to the Young Questors, on a bus and a train and a bus, every Friday night. I went to this theatre club for five years and was in lots of plays.

me getting ready to go on stage in Much Ado About Nothing by William Shakespeare

By the time I got to university, I'd spent most of my life either writing plays, being in plays, directing plays, performing **sketches** or doing comedy.

I wrote two or three plays at university, which were put on. One of them, called *Backbone*, was about my family, and that got performed at the Royal Court Theatre in London when I was about 21. It was pretty exciting having my play put on in London, but – and I know this will sound crazy – I never really got used to all these people coming to see it. It always felt a bit weird. I suppose I couldn't believe all these strangers wanted to see my play!

THE ENGLISH STAGE COMPANY
presents

BACKBONE
By MICHAEL ROSEN

OPENED AT THE ROYAL COURT THEATRE
ON MAY 8th 1968

premièred by the English Stage Society in a production without decor on 11th February and repeated on the 18th, 1968

Photo by Douglas Jeffery

BACKBONE

MICHAEL ROSEN

Royal Court Theatre

the Backbone *programme*

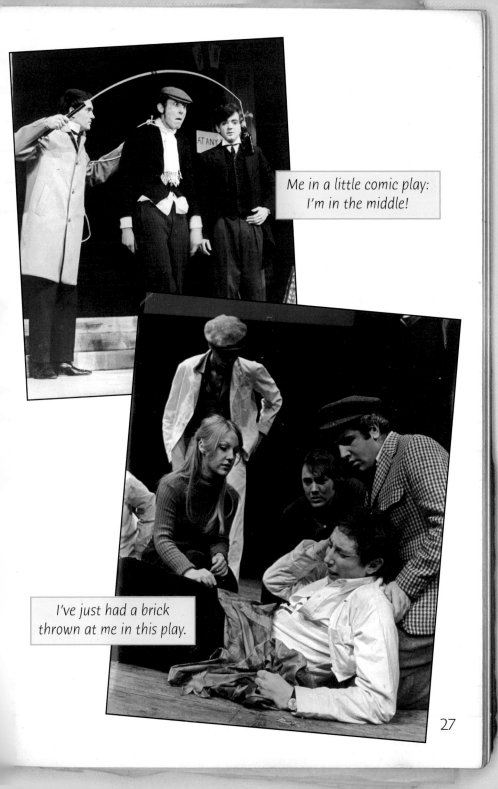

Me in a little comic play:
I'm in the middle!

I've just had a brick
thrown at me in this play.

27

In my last year or two at university I wanted to work in theatre.
I wanted to be a mixture of a director, actor and writer.
But in the end I got

me, after I left university

distracted and instead of going into theatre, I joined the BBC.

I got a job as a **producer** and director working in radio and television and wrote plays and **documentaries** and worked on a TV programme for young children, called *Playschool*.

This is Johnny Ball.
I directed him when
I worked on Playschool.
That meant making
sure the cameras
showed him properly.

I left the BBC after three years and went back to college to study film.

From the age of 16, I'd been writing all the time, a mixture of poems, stories, plays and sketches – I was interested in all those different kinds of writing. But it wasn't until I left the BBC that I started really focusing on my poems.

Mum'll be coming home today,
~~tet.~~ It's three weeks she's been away,
When dad's alone
all we eat
is cold meat
which I don't like
And he burns the toast I want just-brown,
and I _hate_ taking the ash-can down.

He's mended the door
from the little fight,
on Thursday night,
so it doesn't show,
And can we have grilled tomatoes,
Spanish onions and roast potatoes,
And will you sing me "I'll never more roam"
When I'm in bed, when you've come home.

Nov'.66.

for mum.

This poem was eventually published.

"I wish I could write a poem like that"

My mum and dad loved poetry. They used to read it and listen to it on the radio, and they had recordings of poetry that they used to play, so there had always been quite a lot of talk about poetry going on in the house.

CLASS 3
MAGAZINE

"THE TIME HAS COME," THE WALRUS SAID,
"TO TALK OF MANY THINGS,
OF SHOES AND SHIPS AND SEALING WAX,
OF CABBAGES AND KINGS,
AND WHY THE SEA IS BOILING HOT,
AND WHETHER PIGS HAVE WINGS."

JULY
1956

My first poem was printed inside this magazine.

I was about 11 when I wrote my first poem. It was about a train slowing down, which is possibly the most boring subject you could ever try to write a poem about. It shouldn't be, because you can write a poem about absolutely anything. Anyway, it was printed in a little magazine and I was quite proud of it, but I remember my parents getting excited about a poem written by a girl in my class. Her poem was about a windmill and I remember thinking, "I wish I could write a poem that my parents would get excited about."

31

When I was about 15 or 16 I read a book called *A Portrait of the Artist as a Young Man* by James Joyce. At the beginning James Joyce writes about the things he did when he was a boy, and he writes it in the voice of the child he was then. So he's pretending to be a child as he writes, and I thought, "Wow – I'd like to do that." So when I was 16, I started writing about when I was a boy, in the voice of a child.

I also started reading poems by a poet called Gerard Manley Hopkins. He writes very difficult poems. Sometimes he changes the English language to try and make it say what he wants to say, and I thought I'd like to write poems like that too.

Practising writing poems: the little lines above the words are me counting the beats in each line.

xliii s   XXN

I share my bedroom with my brother
and I don't like it.
His bed's by the window
under my map of England's railways
that has a hole in just above Leicester
where Tony Sanders, he says,
killed a Roman centurion
with the Radio Times.

My bed's in the corner
and the paint on the skirting-board
wrinkles when I push it with my thumb
which I do sometimes when I go to bed
sometimes when I wake up
but mostly on Sundays
when we stay in bed all morning

That's when he makes pillow-dens
under the blankets
so that only his left eye shows
and when I go deep-bed mining
for elastoplast spools

that I scatter with my feet
the night before,
and I jump on to his bed
shouting: eegracey oureyourcess
heaping pillows on his head:
"now breathe, now breathe"
and then there's quiet and silence
so I pull it away quick
and he's there laughing all over
sucking fresh-air
along his breathing-tube fingers.

Actually, sharing's alright.

Dec/Jan
66/67

an early draft of a poem

Each poem would take me days to write. I'd rush home and work away at it. I'd do four or five **drafts** and never be satisfied. I'd often get stuck in the middle of writing, or not be able to finish a poem, or when I did finish it, I'd think it was no good. It was a way of training, really. Just as when a carpenter learns how to make a table, I was learning that you don't just get satisfied with using any old word – that you have to try again and try again, until you actually get to what it is that you want to say.

By the time I was about 22 or 23, I had a pile of poems about when I was a boy, and I started sending them off to publishers. At first no one was interested, but eventually I was put in touch with an editor who really liked them. She got me together with an illustrator – Quentin Blake. Yes, the now world-famous Quentin Blake. He illustrated the book, and when I saw the poems next to his pictures, I was very excited.

Quentin is, I think, a mime artist on the page. When he sees the shape of someone's body, he seems to say to himself, "That means happiness," or "That means panic," or "That means worry," and he can draw that feeling in the shape of someone's body, just as when you play **charades**. I can hand over my writing to him and just say, "Do it whatever way you like," because I know I'll always like what he does.

the great Quentin Blake

The Sleepy Baby-sitter's Curse

Oh naked bone shine
faff and pander
go to dead –
thistle stalk linen legs.
Why o why
will he never go through bed?

Rustle Me Lamkin
O creep, O crawl, O pillow fall
wind it, bind it
wrap it, mind it
why o why o why
won't he grow.

Nows the wrestle now
one last rattlescome
sting it antwerp
sting it coxcomb
I'll zero. I'm warning. I'll zero
H.Q. – O.K. Zero and out.
Thanks H.Q.

Goodnightgoodnightgoodnightgoodnight.

90   91

Here it is in print: my first published
book of children's poems.

I share my bedroom with my brother
and I don't like it.
His bed's by the window
under my map of England's railways
that has a hole in just above Leicester
where Tony Sanders, he says,
killed a Roman centurion
with the Radio Times.

My bed's in the corner
and the paint on the skirting board
wrinkles when I push it with my thumb
which I do sometimes when I go to bed
sometimes when I wake up
but mostly on Sundays
when we stay in bed all morning.

That's when he makes pillow dens
under the blankets
so that only his left eye shows
and when I go deep-bed mining
for elastoplast spools
that I scatter with my feet
the night before,
and I jump on to his bed
shouting: eeyoueeyoueeeyouee
heaping pillows on his head:
'Now breathe, now breathe'
and then there's quiet and silence
so I pull it away quick
and he's there laughing all over
sucking fresh air along his breathing-tube fingers.

Actually, sharing's all right.

66   67

35

Ideas about ideas

Well, all that was in the early 1970s and of course I'm still writing. I write something nearly every day. Sometimes it's writing like this, other times it's a whole poem, sometimes it's just a bit of a poem.

The last poem I wrote was about being in a hotel room with my kids and there was a daddy-long-legs flying about the room. The children wanted me to kill it. "Kill it, Dad, kill it!" But I didn't kill it, and when we turned out the light the daddy-long-legs was still in the room. Then in the morning, when we got up, we went into the bathroom and the daddy-long-legs was dead on the floor.

You see, I never get it right first time.

I was writing about the sound the
daddy-long-legs made when it hit
the lampshade – it went
tut-a-tutter-tut-a-tutter –
and I thought, that sounds like jazz
music, which I really like. And suddenly

I had another idea. (This is what happens
when you write poems: you get ideas
about ideas!) The *tut-a-tutter-tut-a-*
tutter could become the **chorus** of the
poem. And remembering how
the daddy-long-legs was laid out
on the tiles in the morning, legs
splayed and silent, gave me
the last line: "The jazz is over."

That grew out of sitting there, and thinking
and thinking and thinking about what
something is really, really like.
And though that was only two days ago it's
not that much different to what
I was doing when I was 16.

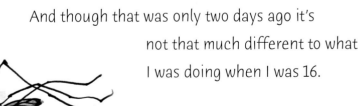

"Read me!"

Poets make their poems interesting by making familiar things seem unfamiliar. In a way, above every word in a poem, there's a poet waving a flag, saying, "Read me! This is really interesting!"

There's lots of ways poets can do this. They can be musical – making the words into a rhythm. Or they can show you how one thing is like another – like how the daddy-long-legs hitting his legs on the lampshade sounds like jazz music. Or they can put in a strange word, a word you hadn't expected.

Going back to writing the daddy-long-legs poem, I thought, "There's something about daddy-long-legs – they've got whiskers, like cat's whiskers." I liked that word, so I wrote it down and then I thought, "There's an echoing word that's to do with whiskers and the sound a daddy-long-legs makes: whispers." So later in the poem, I used the word whispers.

In every poem there are what I call "secret strings" that run between words and phrases. These secret strings can come from the rhythm, the rhyme, the way the pictures or "images" are linked, or from the sounds of words hooking together.

The wish-dasher

Because my mum and dad could speak, between them, **Yiddish**, French, German, Latin, bits of Russian and bits of Italian, the house was full of language play. Also, my dad was very fond of playing with words and language, often in a slightly rude way!

So when I see funny headlines in the newspapers, where they've played around with words, that seems to me the kind of thing that my dad, my brother or my mum would do. For example, the dishwasher broke down when I was about 20 and my mum stopped calling it a dishwasher and started calling it a "wish-dasher" – it dashes your wishes because it's broken down!

Playing with language is fun and can produce some pretty silly poems – I've always enjoyed writing these sorts of poems because I'm often in a nutty mood and enjoy messing about.

Here's an example of me in a nutty mood: I like raisins,
I absolutely adore raisins, I'm just completely addicted to
raisins. In fact, it's slightly mad that I love raisins as much
as I do. If there are no raisins in the house I get a bit twitchy.
So, in our house, quite often there are raisins in packets,
in jars, in little plastic boxes from the local Turkish
supermarket. I have them with every meal, a few raisins.
And I play a game with my kids where I put my hand into
the raisin jar and I pretend to *be* a raisin. I shout in a muffled
voice as if I'm inside the raisin jar: "Oh, he's gonna pick one
of us, no, no, he's gonna pick me, he's gonna pick me.
No, no! Take me, pick me!" So you can see here,
that I sometimes pretend to be
the things I see around me.
I do this for my seven- and
three-year-old and they
find it quite funny.
"Dad, do the thing with
the jar," they say.

I thought, there's a poem here somewhere, and so I got something along the lines of "A raisin escaped from the raisin jar" as a first line. Then …

It shot across the table like a shooting star.
It leapt in the air like a kangaroo –

But I couldn't get the last line until Elsie, my seven-year-old daughter, helped me, when she said: "Look out, Dad, it's coming for YOU!" So I've got the poem, I've done it, and that came out of mucking about with an idea.

The Sad Book

Not all my poems are funny or silly. My wonderful son, Eddie, died of **meningitis** a few years ago and that's unbelievably difficult for me to cope with.

Eddie at school

For a while I didn't want to write about it at all. But then one day I was standing in

front of some children who'd read my Eddie poems in *Quick Let's Get Out of Here*, and one of them said, "What's Eddie doing now?" and I had to say, straight away, "He died." Then somebody said, "What did he die of?" and I had to say, "Meningitis." In a way, that opened a little lid in me. I had a picture in my mind of explaining to that child what had happened to Eddie and what I had thought about it.

Quentin Blake's pictures of Eddie as a toddler, from Quick Let's Get Out of Here

I wrote the *Sad Book* straight out, with hardly any changes in it. One of the great things about writing is that as you write, you find out what you really think. One minute I was angry that he died, the next minute sad. One way in which I've found it possible to cope with what happened to Eddie, is by realising that everybody's sad about something. I'm not different from other people because I'm sad,

I'm the same as other people.

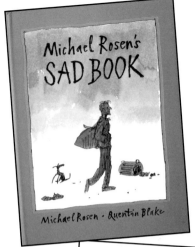

Then I look like this.
And there's nothing I can do about it.

What makes me most sad is when I think about my son Eddie. He died. I loved him very, very much but he died anyway.

Thinking about the way other people are sad really helped me. So, who knows? People might find that reading the *Sad Book*, and talking to other people about the way they're sad, will help them.

What I do now

In any week or month, I will end up writing all sorts of different things. I present a radio programme on BBC Radio 4, so sometimes I have to help write scripts for that.

Quite often, people ask me to write about poetry or books. Then, I like reviewing books for the newspaper. Every now and then, I also experiment with trying to write things that are a bit like plays.

One of the things I've discovered is that I really like all kinds of writing. I love writing articles for magazines, or for websites. I like writing bits of drama and plays. I like writing very serious and sad things. I like writing completely nutty, silly things that make people laugh.

my workroom, with a pair of shoes
I'm trying to get my son to take away

At the moment I have a job that I do as well as writing: I'm the Children's **Laureate**. This means that I'm a kind of **spokesperson** for everyone who writes and publishes children's books. I'm the fifth Children's Laureate and we have each tried to come up with some ideas to help get books into children's hands so that they can read and enjoy them. One of my ideas is to get a kind of children's poetry YouTube up and running on the internet. Another is to help start the Roald Dahl Funny Prize, for the funniest books for children.

the day I was made Children's Laureate

on stage doing some poems

One of the things I love doing most is performing. There's one whole sequence that I do – it's never been written down, but if I were to give it a title, it would be called "Michael's big book of bad things". I act out how, when I was little and I did a bad thing, the next time I did a bad thing, my dad reminded me of the last bad thing I did. And then I go into this whole routine about it. Dad had his favourite bad thing that I did: when I was very small, I threw my mum's best ring out of the window. Of course, this was obviously a matter of some sadness to my dad, because it was never found again, so he would remind me of it, when I was ten or 15, or 20!

Although I'm very busy I do actually find a lot of the work relaxing, because it's what I want to do. To sit down and write about a daddy-long-legs, or a raisin escaping from a raisin jar, is very relaxing because I'm totally absorbed in it. I was staying in a hotel when I wrote about the daddy-long-legs, and instead of watching telly, which some people do to relax, or listening to an iPod, I was writing that.

But there are other things I do in my spare time. I watch quite a lot of football – I support Arsenal – and I like watching international cricket, though, to tell the truth, I will watch anybody if they're playing cricket.

I also like hanging out with the family. I have two young children and we spend a lot of the summer holidays messing about on a beach or in a field.

I've done absolutely everything I could possibly have wanted to do. If you'd said to me when I was 16, "When you're older, people are going to ring you up or write to you and say, 'Will you come to the school and entertain 400 children for an hour?'" I'd have thought, "That's amazing, that's wonderful." If somebody had said, "You could do radio programmes about words and language," I'd have thought, "*What? Me? Really?*" If someone had said, "They're going to invent this thing called the Children's Laureate, a spokesperson for children's books, and you're going to do that," I wouldn't have believed it. Any of it.

on stage in Scotland doing my show

I've ended up doing all the things I love, and I feel very lucky.

Glossary

Biology   the study of living things,
                   especially how their bodies work

charades   a game in which someone acts
                   out a word without saying it, and
                   those watching have to guess what the word is

chorus   groups of words or lines that are repeated at
                   regular intervals within a poem or a song

dissecting   cutting open dead animals or plants in order to
                   study their different parts

documentaries films or radio programmes that are about real life,
                   rather than made-up stories

drafts   different versions of a piece of writing

Latin   the language that was spoken in ancient Rome

Laureate   a person who has been given a special award,
                   usually for being very good at an art or a science

Literature   important pieces of writing by very good writers

meningitis   a serious illness that affects the brain

ponding   fishing in a pond with a little net, to catch and
                   look at the creatures and things that live there

producer   someone who organises the making of a television
                   or radio programme or a film

sketches   very short, funny plays

spectrometer   an instrument for measuring different sorts
                   of light

splayed   spread out awkwardly at odd angles

spokesperson   someone who has been chosen
                   to speak on behalf of a group
                   of people

Yiddish   one of the languages spoken by
                   Jewish people

Index

Timeline: how I became a writer

1946:
I'm born in Harrow, in England.

1953:
I go to West Lodge Middle School, where I love writing stories.

1958:
I join the Questors Theatre club and appear in a lot of plays.

1946 — 1951 — 1953 — 1957 — 1958

1951:
I start school.

1957:
I take the 11-plus exam – and I pass!
I go to grammar school.
I write my first poem. It gets printed in a magazine at school.

CLASS 3
MAGAZINE

"THE TIME HAS COME, "THE WALRUS SAID,
"TO TALK OF MANY THINGS
OF SHOES AND SHIPS AND SEALING WAX,
OF CABBAGES AND KINGS,
AND WHY THE SEA IS BOILING HOT,
AND WHETHER PIGS HAVE WINGS."

JULY
1956

1965:
I move to Wadham College, Oxford, but I'm still not sure I want to be a doctor.

1962:
I study English, French and History at A-level. James Joyce's writing gives me some new ideas for poems.

1968:
My play Backbone is performed at the Royal Court Theatre in London.

1972:
I go back to college to study film, but I'm still working on my poems.

1962   1964 1965 1966   1968 1969   1972   1974

1964:
I start medical school in London – but I discover I don't much like it.

1966:
I switch to study English Literature and Language.

1969:
I get a job at the BBC. I try to get my poems published, but no one is interested.

1974:
At last! My first book of children's poems, Mind Your Own Business, is published.

✦ Ideas for guided reading ✦

Learning objectives: make notes on and use evidence from across a text to explain events or ideas; infer writers' perspectives from what is written and what is implied; reflect on reading habits and preferences and plan personal reading goals; plan and manage a group task over time using different levels of planning

Curriculum links: History: What can we learn about recent history from studying the life of a famous person?

Interest words: Biology, charades, dissecting, documentaries, Laureate, meningitis, spectrometer, splayed, suburb, Yiddish

Resources: poetry by Michael Rosen; ICT; poetry books

Getting started

This book can be read over two or more guided reading sessions.

- As a group, make a list of known facts about Michael Rosen.

- Raise a list of new questions based on these known facts.

- Read the front cover and blurb together. Check that children understand what an *autobiography* is.

Reading and responding

- Read the contents together. Agree the best way to read an autobiography. Do children need to read each chapter in order, or can they dip in?

- Ask children to read to p14, looking for information that is told and information that they can infer.

- As a group, discuss Michael Rosen's memories of his childhood. Was he happy or sad? Well-behaved or mischievous? Distinguish between children's inferences and recall of told information.

- In pairs, ask children to continue reading to p24, making a note of the major events in Michael Rosen's life to this point.